Designs of Darkness

Advanced Tactics in Spiritual Warfare

Paul West

David + Shirley

I pray this book is a blessing to you.

Paul West

Copyright © 2013 Paul West

All rights reserved.

Cover image "The Temptation of Christ" by V. Surikov, 1872.

ISBN-13:
978-1482013528

ISBN-10:
1482013525

Table of Contents

Foreword..v
Author's Preface...vii

1. The Christian Life is a Secret War....................1

2. A Correct Understanding of Christian Victory......9

3. God's Children Grow in the Dark....................17

4. The Design of Worldly Entertainment..............27

5. Beware of Preachers in Darkness...................37

6. Preventing Invasions of Darkness...................47

7. Darkness Defeated Through Humility.............57

FOREWORD

It's been my personal joy to know Paul West for a number of years. I first met him through *Sermon Index,* a website committed to Christ-centered revival. There was an immediate connection in my spirit with Paul because of his deep passion for God and uncompromised commitment to the truths of God's Word. Anything that has ever come from his pen has always brought great blessing and edification. Needless to say, I was overjoyed to learn that Paul was moving beyond just sharing some of his writings on the *Sermon Index* forums and compiling those essays into books.

I am generally of the belief that if you are looking for books to help you plumb the deeper depths of what God offers, you should not waste your time reading contemporary authors. Most would agree that in contrast to the great men and women of God of yesteryear whose writings were weighty and substantive, so much of what lines our bookshelves today is almost frivolous in comparison.

However, **Designs of Darkness** is clearly an exception! This short volume is a treasure trove of truth that merits every believer's time and attention. The author takes a no-nonsense approach to a subject that is sadly lightly considered by modern Christendom. No wonder so many live defeated lives. His insights into the Word of God and his treatment of so important a subject are reminiscent of what you would read by the

Puritans. Paul's ability to craft words and paint pictures is captivating to the reader; but beyond his writing prowess are the solid Biblical truths that every Christian must know in order to live an overcoming life!

In this volume, he turns the light on and exposes the enemy's schemes and deceptions that hold believers in bondage. The author is in dead earnest about the realities of spiritual warfare and the utter importance of knowing and understanding the path to unmitigated and sure victory through Christ. Like a good sermon which will always inform the mind, stir the emotions and challenge the will, reading **Designs of Darkness** will accomplish those same objectives while igniting a fiery passion in your heart to walk in the victory that Christ's death has secured for us.

As a pastor who sees the devastation that sin brings into the lives of those who are defeated by its power, I heartily recommend **Designs of Darkness**. It is an invaluable arsenal providing all that is needed to enable those who engage in battle against the powers of darkness to live victorious Christian lives.

Paul Spuler
Senior Pastor, First Christian Assembly
Burlington, New Jersey

Matt 1:21 "And she will bring forth a Son, and you shall call His name JESUS, for He will save His people from their sins."

Rom. 6:14 – For sin shall not have dominion over you, for you are not under law but under grace.

AUTHOR'S PREFACE

Believers who are weary of defeat and heavy-laden with sin's mastery will find in this publication the solution to their many heartaches and the key to unlocking their long-awaited freedoms in Christ.

Scripture references have been copiously provided and placed mostly at the ends of paragraphs so as to not disrupt the continuity of reading. This should lend itself well for personal study. Admittedly, the food here can at times be weighty, and is thus meant to be digested reflectively and prayerfully and with the Word of God in tandem. The main theme of this book is total deliverance from sin's power and how to arrive at it by overcoming Satan's designs through New Covenant grace. Please note that it is very important to make the distinction between being *saved from sin's power* (Matthew 1:21; Romans 6:14) and the doctrine of *sinless perfection*, which is heresy.

May it please the Father to bless this book to the virgin bride of His Son.

Paul Frederick West
New Braunfels, Texas
April 3, 2013

1 Cor 9:7 - Whoever goes to war at his own expense? Who plants a vineyard and does not eat its fruit? Or who tends a flock and does not drink of the milk of the flock?

2 Cor. 4:7 - But we have this tremendous treasure in earthen vessels, that the excellence of the power may be of God and not of us.

1 Tim 1:18 This charge I commit to you, son Timothy, according to the prophecies previously made concerning you, that by them you may wage a good warfare.

2 Tim. 2:3-4 You therefore must endure hardship as a good soldier of Jesus Christ. No one engaged in warfare entangles himself with the affairs of this life, that he may please him who enlisted him as a soldier.

1. The Christian Life is a Secret War

Philemon 1:2 - To the beloved Apphia, Archippus, our fellow soldier, and to the church in your house.

2 Peter 1:4 by which has been given to us exceedingly great and precious promises, that through these you may be partakers of the divine nature, having escaped the corruption that is in the world thru lust,

The Christian life is a secret war. It is a war unlike any other ever waged in the history of the world, for it is fought upon the hills and valleys of a battlefield which carnal eyes cannot see. The fighting is hidden, the suffering silent. The belligerents are eternal spirit forces manifesting attrition within the temporal canvas of time. All followers of Christ are immediately conscripted into this war upon their new births, and yet not all children of God have taken up arms. These are the conscientious objectors to spiritual aggression, and as a result they do not overcome Satan but remain fleshly defeated and spiritually impotent in the partaking of their Father's Divine Nature. (I Corinthians 9:7; II Corinthians 4:7; I Timothy 1:18; II Timothy 2:3-4; Philemon 1:2; II Peter 1:4)

The soldiers who fight and fall, only to take up arms again and continue fighting are granted measures of ever-increasing light. They are protected by God and enjoy divine rejuvenation daily. Their many wounds are treated; their souls are healed. If they continue to fight and not abandon rank, they are promised food, armor and restored health. They are assured of final victory, though the individual battles are fierce and oftentimes lost. (Psalms 23:3; 34:19; 37:24; 51:12; Proverbs 4:18; 24:16; Isaiah 40:31; Luke 22:32; II Corinthians4:9)

These same soldiers, however, soon discover another most wonderful truth: the lost battles are eventually used to their benefit! Their defeats are found to be designed by God for an ultimately purpose. Through the unfathomable wisdom of God, failure becomes the seedbed from which His children grow in grace as they advance unto perfection through the manifold trials of their faith. The Holy Spirit is given to abide within the bosom of each and every soldier of God's army to point to Jesus Christ and to the ever-blazing light of His holiness. His is a revelatory light. It reveals the designs of darkness; the corrupt strategy of God's foe; the very schemes of Satan. His light prepares the soldier beforehand and equips him with power to overcome in the time of battle. The Holy Spirit is given that the follower of Christ might live a life of perpetual triumph, full of the sweet fragrance of the divine life of Christ and the reality of His everlasting joy. (Song of Solomon 1:3; II Kings 6:8-12; John 15:26; 16:13; Romans 8:28-29; I Corinthians 15:57; II Corinthians 2:14, 16, 9:8; I Timothy 4:15; Hebrews 6:1; I John5:6)

When a man's eyes are opened to the depth and height and length and width of the Lord's love for him, and what it cost God to send Jesus Christ to ransom his soul from hell, this amazing love becomes a great shield by which the fiery darts of Satan are instantly quenched. The Bible declares God's love for His ransomed children to be just as great as His love was for Jesus Christ while He walked the earth. The Word of God declares us to be His eternally-adopted sons and daughters through the precious blood of the New Covenant, the redeemed saints of His own ransomed inheritance, His very own treasure (see John 17:23; Romans 8:39; Ephesians 1:18, 3:18). There is no word in the English language to verbalize or describe the loving endearment between God and His saints in spiritual terms.

Tragically, many saints fighting in the foxholes of righteousness have forgotten these truths. How soon they forget that before they were formed in the womb, God knew them, that He knew the sort of upbringings they would have, the abuse of ungodly influences that would eventually invade their childhoods and steal their innocence. That He would see all their future pain and moral failures, their betrayals of His goodness and their debilitating insecurities that would come as a result.

God partook of their wretched experiences in their entirety, and yet still chose them according to His sovereign pleasure. He invites them now to a most glorious exchange: to know and partake of His own eternal purpose by which they have been created and predestined. This predestined purpose is fulfilled through their conformity to Jesus Christ and in their subsequent justification, sanctification and glorification in Him as they helplessly abide and look unto the Son of God with ever-increasing faith and hope. (Jeremiah 1:5; Galatians 1:15; Ephesians1:5-6;Hebrews2:17)

When we at last come to see our positions of beloved centrality in Christ and the measure of God's compassion for us, the comprehension of our relationship with Him as *"Abba-Father"* will take on a whole new dimension. It will become for us both a shield and salve. God has abundant grace to bind broken hearts through the knowledge His love, sustained even through the worst of our trials and defeats (see Romans 8:38-39), and as we continue to confess and forsake sin, we will soon notice God giving us a greater knowledge of the enemy and the devices he employs to so often stumble and beset us. This tutelage of the Holy Spirit is designed to direct the soldier back to the power of blood of Jesus Christ, to which the sin-mortifying grace of the New Covenant can be ever availed. (Psalm 30:5; Romans 6:14; II Corinthians 2:11; 4:17; Galatians 5:22; Hebrews 9:14; 10:29; I Peter 5:10; I John 1:7; Revelation 12:11)

Secret victories lend to the open fragrance of life in Jesus Christ. *The pinnacle message of this book is that you can overcome all the designs of darkness and be a vessel of deep edification to many.* There is not an enemy in the ranks of Satan which God's grace cannot instantly vanquish. There is not a temptation of the flesh and mind which cannot be broken and cleansed through the holy blood of God. The joy of the soldier never need be broken, even though he may be presently confounded by the powers of darkness. The Lord would encourage us all through these pages to have faith not only in His sovereign compassion pertaining to the restoration of His wounded soldiers, but in the power of His grace in equipping them to overcome the roaring lion's pounce. (II Corinthians 6:10; Philippians 4:4; Ephesians 6:10; II Timothy 2:1; I Thessalonians 5:16; I Peter5:8)

Those who have been chosen of God to radiate the life of His Son in this secret war are given a daily death sentence. This death sentence consists of eclipsing the desires of the flesh so that Christ might have preeminence through their vessels. This measure of flesh-eclipsing is proportionate to the diligence one maintains in walking in the spirit. Walking in the spirit requires a deliberate daily resolve; for it involves a conscientious, collaborative effort with the Holy Spirit in guarding our hearts and minds from evil thought-patterns and ever realigning them Heavenward to where we are seated with Christ in God. (Luke 9:23; John 3:27,30; Romans 8:13; I Corinthians 15:31; II Corinthians 10:5; Colossians 3:5; Hebrews 12:2;IPeter1:13;IJohn5:11)

What many believers do not realize is that the world has been designed by Satan to prevent this realignment. That Satan is the ruler of this world is scripturally uncontested. Through his rule, even the basic God-ordained requirements of food for sustenance and intimacy for procreation have been diabolically perverted via the constant bombardment of advertisements to the flesh. In every corner of the world we find humankind hopelessly entrenched in the satiation of the flesh's lusts. Being dead in sin and blind to the majesty of God, man's habitation is consigned to this dismal plane of Adamic carnality where death reigns through sin.

The grand design of spiritual darkness is to ensure that man's spirit eyes are never opened, and then if they are, never elevated to receive power from the King of Glory to tread the earth in Christ's conquest. If we take too light an approach to this awareness, we can be derailed from this secret war and devoured by the roaring lion who pulls the strings and works the levers of this ruined world. (Genesis 6:5; John 12:31; 14:30; 16:11; Romans 1:24; II Corinthians 4:4; Ephesians 2:2,5; Philippians 3:19;IJohn5:19)

The gaze by which we train our spirits on Him who is altogether lovely is subject to gravity. It takes real effort to resist the pull and maintain a daily loftiness of faith, trust and spiritual integrity toward God. The fight the old saints wrote so prolifically of, and the fearsome war in which the Christian must for a lifetime engage, is not to be found against flesh and blood, but in the maintenance of this unfettered gaze upward.

Devils and charlatan preachers, humanistic philosophies and man's intransigent quest for money are just some of the many lead weights used by the enemy to sink our minds down into the dregs of carnal rapport. When the mind becomes preoccupied with fleshly pursuits, the vibrancy of communion between our spirits and His becomes eclipsed. Darkness then prevails upon light and the soldier is drawn out from the safety of the Cleft of Christ and into the open battlefield where he is soon ensnared by the baitings of his own lust. (Song of Solomon 5:16; Matthew 7:15; I Corinthians 10:4; Galatians 5:16, 19-21; Ephesians 6:12; Colossians 2:8; James 1:14; I Timothy 6:10; II Timothy2:22;IIPeter2:1)

God's adopted children through the Second Adam are intended to be fruitful and multiply and have dominion over all the earth, sky and sea like the original Adam. But the fruitfulness of this New Covenant is that of the Holy Spirit, the multiplication is in the discipleship of new fruit-bearers, and the dominion is in their overcoming of the cares of world, the lusts of the flesh and the schemes of the devil. This book was written to expose Satan's lures and to show how God's soldiers might exercise dominion over all the wiles of this already-defeated foe. But before we begin this marvelous exhortation, it is paramount that we first have a clear understanding of what the true, victorious Christian life really is. (Genesis 1:26; I Corinthians 15:45-49; Galatians 5:22-23; Ephesians 5:9; Colossians 3:12)

2. A Correct Understanding of Christian Victory

A large part of the New Testament deals with spiritual warfare, with armor, with refreshing, rejuvenation, with prevailing over the enemy by the blood of Jesus Christ and dominion over sin's power through grace. God clearly wants us to live our lives to where we are constantly overcoming fear, the love of money, discouragement, bad moods, criticism, sexual lust, pride, unrighteous anger. Victory over these must be our testimony. A preacher must be able to preach deliverance from sin's power with boldness and certainty, and a Bible teacher must be able to show believers through the Word of God how to overcome Satan. And both the preacher and teacher must be able to demonstrate the actuality of this victory by the fruit of the Spirit in their own walks and family life. (John 8:32; Romans 8:37; I Corinthians 15:57; Ephesians 6:11; I Timothy 3:9; Revelation12:11)

To confound the haughty wisdom of the world, Jesus calls only the weary and heavy-laden, and not the strong and able to victory. He calls only the defeated and thirsty. He calls only the hungry, the helpless, the diseased in spirit to rest. All who are tired of suffering under the tyranny of sin He calls to Himself, and these soon find blessed deliverance. He makes all things new. He opens wide the prison doors and sets besieged spirits free and aflame with God's love (Isaiah 61:1).

The freedom He grants is absolute, His love unspeakable, His joy ever-abounding. He invites all with ears to hear and hearts to yearn to come unto Him and die and be resurrected with His divine nature. He offers a winning, joyous life, full of His overcoming grace and triumph, a foretaste of heaven on earth through the earnest of the Holy Spirit. There can never be anyone with any excuse to not be willing to be made willing to become a candidate for this glorious calling. (Matthew 5:3, 11:28; John 12:24; Romans 1:20; I Corinthians 1:26-28; II Corinthians1:22;5:17;IIPeter1:4)

Conversely, the further a Christian drifts from Christ and declines this calling, the longer the shadows begin to grow as the light of God abates in his life. If we notice shadows elongating in our lives, we must check our proximity to Christ. It is never a matter of our own willful resistance to evil, for as empty voids we cannot resist the darkness. True victory consists of returning to the Light of Christ, for it is from the Light of His Life alone which darkness flees. (John 1:5, 8:12, 15:5)

Many believers have a wrong understanding of Christian victory. They think victory is an unbroken span of sinless perfection where one does not transgress in word, thought or deed. But this is an inaccurate picture of triumph. True victory in Christ which leads from glory to glory is found in overcoming temptation through the instant obtainment of God's grace in confessing and forsaking ungodly impulses as they enter our mind to defile the conscience and conceive sin. There is not a Christian alive who is immune from confessing the impurity of some internal revelation of unchristlikeness by the Holy Spirit, in accordance to the current light of their own level of sanctification. (Psalms 84:7; II Corinthians 3:18; Philippians 3:12-21;James1:15;IJohn1:8;2:1)

The Holy Spirit is always faithful to bring the knowledge of sin to the understanding of God's children. This is the purpose of light. Christian victory, therefore, is found just as much in the resistance of darkness as it is in the returning to the light. Every Christian is able, in some capacity, to resist darkness in the face of the light he or she currently has. The problem arises when one enters into varying degrees of darkness minus the corresponding grace of God. A believer may be plagued with a sense of his or her own impurity, and yet, the inward act of opposing and confessing the impurity constitutes one victorious before God. This victory is granted through the overcoming power of God's grace and the instantaneous effect of Christ's blood-cleansing through faith. (John 16:8; I Corinthians 10:3; 14:24; II Corinthians 2:19; Philippians 3:16; Hebrews 4:12;IIPeter2:9)

It is therefore not the person who hides an outbreak of sin who is counted victorious, for these efforts of flesh-quenching are but a mere masking; a mortal concealment, a clever corking of a fierce volcanic eruption occurring deep beneath the surface of the skin. It is not the believer who plugs the volcano, but he who flees from the lava as it threatens to burn his conscience who is counted truly victorious. Such a man needs no plug for the volcano, for the gracious blood of Christ is able to make the fire recede. The instantaneous effect of grace is one of cooling, one of healing, one of fire-recession, one of utter cleansing and instant restoration. (Matthew 11:29; Luke 11:39; Ephesians 2:13; Hebrews 4:3; 9:14; I John 1:9)

The period between the rises of these volcanic impulses and their abatements are what present a sense of triumph to the child of God as he continually walks in the Spirit of Christ. Without these, the cork of the law is needed to stop the volcano from erupting through the flesh. This corking via the law is where many believers become weary and heavy-laden, scalded by the lava and having fallen prey to legalistic teachings which thrive through the self-condemnation of failed human willpower(Colossians2:23).

To avoid the pitfalls of legalism, the child of God must have an understanding of the power of Christ's blood and how it relates to victory by grace through faith. The sooner this truth is appropriated, the sooner the cork of the law can be rendered obsolete. *How we regard the cork is, in fact, all the difference between the Old Covenant and the New Covenant.* The instant cooling of the uncorked volcano should be the normal condition for all New Covenant believers. But even then, those who suffer burning should recognize the pain of failure is often the Father's way of making the cross even more precious, more attractive and more needful through the employment of fiery trials. Do not new seedlings soon spring forth through the burnt ground of a forest? Likewise, victory in the spirit of a believer is restored when the heart is humbled unto confession and the conscience cleansed in the justifying blood of Christ. (Rom.5:3,4,9;IPeter4:12-13; Heb.10:22)

The more the Christian grows in grace, the more he learns of how the power of the blood of Jesus works in conjunction with the power of the Holy Spirit. The Holy Spirit is ever-faithful to alert the conscience of impending volcanic eruptions. He shows us our sin in the darkness for it to be crucified in the light. If the conscience happens to get burnt during times of sin-discovery, we must not allow ourselves to come under condemnation, but instead confess the burn immediately! Let this practice become a habit, and we will be well on our way to greater revelations in the Word, anointing in our ministries, and extended sojournings in victory (Matthew 10:27; Romans 8:1).

When thinking of the principles of Christian victory I am often reminded of the Scottish biologist who inadvertently discovered penicillin in 1928 when he noticed a radius of destroyed bacteria surrounding a piece of mold in a plate culture. This famous epiphany in science is a spiritual parallel of the arming of the mind of Christ to the inhibition of fleshly lusts. In the same way harmful microbes cannot proliferate within the proximity of penicillin, so the lusts of the flesh cannot spiritually colonize within the vessel of a child of God who is armed with the mind of Christ (Galatians 5:16-18).

The "armament" of the mind in the Bible is based upon a Greek term for weapon. It denotes an ancient warrior holding a shield and javelin, ready to go to war. In this context, the Christian does battle against the lusts of the flesh which war against the soul (I Peter 2:11; 4:1). The soldier who is not armed for this conflict will soon be overrun and infected by the advancing troops which seek to draw out the lusts of his flesh. To guard the mind against the bacteria of sin, it must be daily renewed and armed in Christ. But how, it may be asked, is this to be accomplished experientially?

A consideration of death must occur in the principle of self to where the overcoming life of Another Power is activated. This death is reckoned through the believer's own identification in Christ's death (Romans 6:3). The result is an internal submission to the mortifying influence of the Holy Spirit's power over the will of the flesh. Therefore, if people who have not yet been baptized into this death can hear the gospel preached, and lift their hands and shout hallelujah, it is a false gospel. For the true gospel breaks before it heals, accuses before it acquits, crucifies before it resurrects.

Every Christian must be daily crucified to overcome the onslaught of spiritual contaminates seeking to enter his mind and heart through the designs of darkness. We must allow the Word of God to thoroughly dwell in us and rule our hearts from the place and peace of death. If we would be more than conquerors, we must attune our hearts to obey the Spirit's soft dealings of death. As lone pieces of mold amidst perverse colonies of bacteria, we must come to see ourselves as dead on the plate but alive to God who infuses our dead bodies with the grace and faith and power and overcoming life of the resurrected Lord Jesus Christ (Romans 6:11). We can kill an Egyptian with our bare hands and hide him in the sand, or we can allow God to sink the entire Egyptian army to the bottom of the ocean. One is a picture of covertly striving against sin through fleshly effort, in which any legalistic victory we gain is upon shifting, foundationless sand. The other is a picture of God's triumphant grace, absolute and sure, with sin's dominion cast to the ocean's floor. (Exodus2:12;Micah7:19)

Man is a match, made to be struck with death so he can be burst aflame with the conquering Life of Christ. This is the reality of New Covenant victory, and the way which God brings triumph to His children! *"...as Christ hath suffered for us in the flesh, arm yourselves likewise with the same mind: for he that hath suffered in the flesh hath ceased from sin; That he no longer should live the rest of his time in the flesh to the lusts of men, but to the will of God"* (I Peter 4:1-2).

3. God's Children Grow in the Dark

"Rejoice not against me, O mine enemy: when I fall, I shall arise; when I sit in darkness, the LORD shall be a light unto me. I will bear the indignation of the LORD, because I have sinned against him, until he plead my cause, and execute judgment for me: he will bring me forth to the light, and I shall behold his righteousness." (Micah 7:8-9)

If God's ways are not according to human logic, this truth is nowhere more evident than in the way He grows His children in sanctification and wisdom during times of failure and defeat. Saplings sprout from the earth under direct sunlight and in optimal temperatures; but in contrast to this, God's children grow in times of darkness, in the midst of trials and tests. They are refreshed in the sunlit presence of the Lord with spiritual reprieve and rejuvenation – but they grow in holiness and sanctification in the dark. As seeds germinate beneath soil, and babies are knit together in the darkness of their mothers' wombs, so the Lord fashions our spiritual bones and substance together in dark wombs of affliction. Did not Samson's hair re-grow after his eyes had been put out? Did not God recapture Jonah's obedience while he lay in the dark belly of a whale? Was it not from the darkness of the wilderness that Jesus came forth with the Holy Spirit upon Him with power to set the captives free? And did not Almighty God form the earth within the void of created darkness, before the initial command of light? (Genesis 1:3; Judges 16:21-22; Jonah 2:1-10;Luke4:14)

Look at an earthly child. He eats and plays during the day, when sunlight encompasses his world. But at night, while sleeping, the food he ate miraculously transforms into bone and muscle. It is in the darkness of sleep and in the cocoon of sunless dormancy where his physical growth takes place, and to the extent that when he awakens, he is noticeably taller and his features all the more defined and mature. All parents have observed this bittersweet metamorphosis in their children.

God's children grow spiritually in the dark as well. The wisdom of God allows the enemy's designs of darkness to be used in the perfecting of Christ-conformity, in fulfillment of Romans

8:28. It is in the dark cocoon of trials and difficulties where a Christian's brilliant colors formed, and where the wings of faith are made to bring him to the throne of grace. This is why we are taught not to despise the chastening and correction of the Lord, and why we are to embrace His rod in the furnace of chastisement and in the allowance of fleshly temptations (Proverbs 3:11).

It is in the fire where the precious metals of earth gain their worth in the estimation of men. The Christian, likewise, is tempered and seasoned and grown in inhospitable atmospheres which seem unfruitful for the furtherance of his value. We know our that righteous Father forever seeks the utmost good for His children; we must therefore endure His blessed rod of purification and never doubt His supreme love while suffering in the face of our seasonal pain (I Peter 1:6; 4:12). Remember this blessed truth the next time you fail in His grace. The night cometh; the fire is kindled - and our suffering in the flesh is God's will for the promotion of Christ's Life in our vessels. The flesh suffers so the precious elements of the spirit can come forth like gold (I Peter 1:7).

Enter then into God's appointed chamber of growth with weeping and mourning over your own unprofitable resolutions, with your myriad of failures, and all your broken aspirations to please Him. But in the midst of these, know that God's plans for your life are not negated in the least within the cocoon of darkness, but rather forged upon the anvil of your suffering in the flesh. If you trust Him, He will see you though the fiery furnace and you will come out the other end without a strand of hair singed. He will hold you in His mighty Hand while you sleep, and when the sun finally rises, you will have grown. And your growth will be noticeable to all. (Daniel 3:25-27; I Timothy4:15)

The lowly caterpillar resigns to the darkness of the cocoon only to fly away in the light of liberation and on the wings of beauty. As the worm's freedom was perfected in a lair of darkness, so God's strength is made perfect through the chamber of suffering. Allow God keep you in this chamber until you can reckon by faith your actual death in Christ and come into the glorious knowledge of His grace. His plan for your life is to adorn you with the beauty of Christ; to mint you with His life, and to impart His divine nature in you to such a degree that you might fly above all the darkness of sin and Satanic bondage of the earth's pull. (Romans 6:6-11; II Corinthians 2:19;Colossians3:3;IIPeter1:4)

Sometimes a believer will fail a test of God and enter into a season of darkness. Perhaps he was living a life of victory, walking with a clean conscience before God and enjoying the resources of Christ when a temptation hit, overwhelmed him, took away his peace and snuffed his joy. Prior to this, he thought he was strong; he thought he could resist the temptation as he had many times in the past (I Corinthians 10:12). He had been walking in the Spirit that morning; by the evening, however, he finds himself cast down and once again in the dregs of a besetting sin. Because he loathes himself to such a degree, there is a great reluctance to be recovered before God. This is because he is made to feel he is fighting a hopeless cause, and that his Christianity is just not "working", despite knowing and experiencing all the verses and truths pertaining to the divine nature in overcoming sin. Satan is quick to invade his mind during these moments and convince him that any continuation of walking with God is futile.

We must be encouraged with the truth of all-loving, all-wise Father who allows certain things to happen for the furtherance of our good. Never an instigator of sin, we know from scripture that God will at times allow the tempter of souls to strike at the hearts of His children for a specific cause. The Holy Spirit led Jesus into the wilderness specifically to be tested by Satan; Jesus foretold of Peter's allowance to be sifted by request of Satan; Satan asked to destroy all which righteous Job held in possession, and God granted all of these (Luke 22:31).

God will allow the designs of darkness to try us as well. When He permits the enemy to strike, a strong presentation to engage in evil will come to our minds. It comes as an invitation to rebel against the light God has already given us on the subject by which we are currently being tempted. Previously, we could hold our ground and resist it with resolve – but now it crashes upon the shores of our mind like a tsunami, catching us off guard. The powers of darkness are opportunistic in this regard: they wait until the mind is weak and the flesh is strong enough to overpower the spirit's restraining grace. When the moment is right, they pounce.

When a believer fails God, he fails against the will of his inner man (Romans 7:22-25; Galatians 5:17; I John 3:9; 5:8). He so loathes sin, yet in those dire moments he feels himself at once helplessly dominated by the flesh. It is never the Lord's will that we fail during these times of testing, but if we do fail, He foreknew and still permitted it. It's difficult for us to compute God allowing an event to transpire, knowing it will cause us to sin. But didn't He already know Peter would deny Christ - and being fully able to prevent it, chose instead to allow Peter's failure? Yes. This is because the Lord had a great lesson to teach Peter – a lesson which could only be acquired in the darkness of despair brought on by his fall (Luke22:32).

The Lord is not an earthly teacher. An earthly teacher, when she gives a test, does not know her pupils' grades until after the test is taken. But God knows all the grades beforehand, yet still administers the test in order to teach His children the subject of grace in a supremely profound way. The reason God allows such tests is to demonstrate to us that only Christ can pass them. When we fail a test in God's school, it is because we took it ourselves and did not allow Christ to take the test for us. A failing grade always indicates an insufficiency of grace. The great end of all God's testing in allowing the devil to sift us is to amplify the righteousness of Jesus Christ, destroy all boasting, and convince us of the necessity of Holy Spirit empowerment for living the Christian life. (Romans 8:3; Philippians 4:13; Colossians 1:11; Hebrews 10:8)

When we take a test and fail, our eyes are usually blind to the fact that we took the test ourselves. There is a reluctance to look up to God because of our sense of hopelessness. A defeatist mindset encompasses us and we begin to see ourselves as worthless subjects (II Corinthians 2:7). Ah! But this is precisely the reason why the Teacher of teachers administered the test! *It is to foster within us the very understanding that we are unable to master the subject matter apart from Christ.* An earthly teacher introduces the subject matter to her students for them to comprehend it on the test; God, in contrast, uses the test's incomprehensibility to demonstrate the subject matter to His children. And the subject matter is always grace through Jesus Christ. These lessons of grace are often learnt in a dark classroom, with Satan as God's appointed proctor and disciplinarian over the test material. (Luke 22:31; I Corinthians 5:5; II Cor. 12:7)

When we fail a test and are in the dark, God would have us get up immediately and continue on in faith. Our Father wills that after each failure we would approach the blood of Christ through confession and be instantly restored. He calls us to look into His Word to see how and why we flunked. The Word of God is like a mirror which sits upon a wash-basin filled with Christ's blood (James 1:23). It is in this mirror we are to look, confess, and wash. That is His remedial program. When we fail any test, we return to this basin. The more we approach it by way of humility and the will to master the test's subject matter, the more we are transformed by the power and wisdom of the Holy Spirit. (James 3:17; Hebrews 12:11; I Peter 5:6)

Always remember this: at anytime, if we rise high enough in the air above even the most fiercest and darkest of storms, we shall find the sun shining in the midst of a cloudless, blue sky. *When Satan descends, the child of God must ascend.* The Old Covenant's realm is beneath the sun where nothing is new and all is vanity; the New Covenant beckons and empowers us through grace to sail forever beyond the sun, where all things are new and the everlasting joy of the Lord abounds (Ecclesiastes1:2).

Never stay down after you flunk a test in God's school. Pick yourself up in the dark and go immediately to the mirror of God's Word and wash in the fountain of Christ's blood. If the Lord sees you have begun to leave your first love, or have forgotten how He cleansed you from your former sins, these may warrant an exam to where you suddenly find yourself in a chamber of seasonal darkness in order to deflate your budding pride (II Peter 1:9; Revelation 2:4). Embrace God's rod in these circumstances – but do not stay down in the dark. The subject matter He is teaching you is employment of His grace through a return to humility. The purpose for all His tests is to teach us the impossibility of passing any of them save for the grace of Christ manifest in us.

Christians are most vulnerable to fail a test when they have been most victorious under the illusion of pride. We must therefore stay forever low before the Master, and never forget that the Authorship of any victory we experience is always His (Hebrews 12:2).

4. The Design of Worldly Entertainment

The design of worldly entertainment is in the usurpation of spiritual joy. Entertainment is but a decoy, a glass diamond, a nugget of fool's gold in exchange for the true riches found only in Jesus Christ. The enemy waits for the joy of the Lord to abate in believers before presenting them with the sham of entertainment and worldly amusements. The powers of darkness observe God's children and watch for signs of diminishment in their spiritual rejuvenation; they observe the quality of devotion and spy on their quiet times with God. When the occasion is ripe to offer the apple of entertainment, they do so, and like Ehud and Joab, slip the knife deceptively into the belly of the soul (Judges 3:20-22; II Samuel 20:10).

As the poison of entertainment begins its

spread, the joy of the Lord is replaced by visceral delight. And as the child of God flounders here, the powers of darkness strike a second time. Here they strike with a delusional acceptance that soulish entertainment might be successfully married to God's spiritual joy. Like Naaman the Syrian, they find themselves meandering between two temples: the shrine of a false god and the temple of the true God (II Kings 5:18; Matthew 6:24). A profane altar is erected within the tabernacle of the Holy Spirit, the believer's heart is commandeered, and the incense of the flesh is burnt in lieu of the Sprit's fire.

The power of soul entertainment and the influence it has over the flesh (if not overcome by spiritual joy) has an electrifying draw, and, in the end, detrimental consequences to the "new man" created in us. Entertainment and joy cannot co-exist for long, and entertainment will always win the fight over joy for dominion in the heart when the mind continues to be set on carnal endeavors (Luke 12:19). The powers of darkness know this truth very well, which is why the world has been designed to be a lair of entertainment, a colossal web to entrap men and women for the purpose of euthanizing their minds from the realities of God and the impending doom of eternal judgment and hell.

To effectively counter the dagger of entertainment, the mind's loins must be girded and set upon the glory of Jesus Christ. The believer must pray for God to foster within him a new mindset adaptation, to shift the gaze of his faith from earth to heaven (Hebrews 12:2; I Peter 1:13). We must learn to recognize when the shadows are drawing longer and our inner men are beginning to hunger. And upon this recognition, to fly to the blood of Jesus Christ where God has provided light, food and shelter for our beleaguered spirits (I John 1 :5,7,9). Any hesitation to fly to Christ in these moments puts our spirit men in jeopardy of being outmatched by the fake glitter and false gold of worldly entertainment and vain amusements.

Consider the lure of money. A man's success in life is not to be measured by the height of his salary or the fatness of his possessions, but by the depth of his yieldedness to God. Can a believer chase after money and still serve God? According to Jesus, the simultaneous pursuit of money and God is impossible. And not only that, the believer who loves money will eventually come to hate God. It is good to examine ourselves in this respect. Are our minds forever focused on increasing our salaries and getting newer and bigger and better possessions? Are we discontent with what God in His wisdom has allotted us on earth? An archangel in heaven once wanted more than what God had allotted for his station, and his lust for more transformed him into a devil in an instant. (Isaiah 14:12-14; Matthew 6:24; Luke 12:15; I Timothy 6:6-10)

We need to see that the love of money is satanic at its core, for it reflects an inward boost of pride, of thankless discontent and damnable self-rule. This is a trait Adam inherited from Satan, and was spread to us all who were in his loins when he bowed the knee to the serpent. All who run after materialism and earthly wealth subconsciously despise God's plans and are in intrinsic opposition to the will of their Creator. No wonder Jesus said it is easier for a camel to go through the eye of a needle than for a rich man to enter the Kingdom of Heaven! If we think we are immune from this deception, we must remember: a deceived person does not know he is deceived until brings the counterfeit note to the bank. And by then it is too late to avoid exposure and prosecution. (Psalm 119:36; Proverbs 23:4; Matthew 19:34; Romans 5:12; Colossians3:5;Hebrews13:5)

Because our minds are naturally poised toward earth-bound objects and passions, an effective strategy employed by spiritual wickedness is to constantly provide diversions and distractions to keep the follower of Christ from heavenly pursuits (Luke 21:34; I Corinthians 7:35; I Peter 2:11). The world in which we live is replete with such a myriad of alluring vanities, fruitless enticements and empty attractions as to make each inch of our sojourning here a potential bog to gratify our insatiable intellect and electrify the flesh. To effectively circumnavigate these bogs, diligence is required in obtaining knowledge of God's grace to withstand Satan and maintain an unmolested mind on our stalwart path to heaven (II Corinthians 2:14; Philippians 4:8; Hebrews4:16;IIPeter3:18).

These distractions at first present themselves in small increments. Initially they are but the polyps that forewarn of cancer if not excised upon detection. They appear benign (that is, some harmless divergence from the narrow path of holiness); but are, in fact, strategically-designed weapons used by the enemy to infiltrate our minds and set down destructive roots. The invasion's purpose is to create a mental fortress which seeks to strangle the life of one's inner devotion to God.

The reason we find it so difficult to pray, to read God's Word, and to engage our minds in spiritual meditation for prolonged periods of time is because invisible spirit powers and principalities surround us and war against these efforts. Their mission is to keep our spirits from making contact with God to gain strength by the power of His Spirit (Ephesians 3:16). Believers who live for righteousness and who seek to be transformed by God will be mercilessly persecuted by these evil forces, for such believers wrestle not against flesh and blood, but with demons. These sinister forces seek to desensitize believers over a period of time through minuscule doses of compromise to where at last the child of God crumbles under a flaming arrow and yields to sin. (Ephesians6:12;IITimothy3:12)

When the arrow strikes the mind, it sticks and infects. The poison defiles the believer's conscience and immediately establishes a root in the heart. The bow from which the arrow is propelled is most commonly strung by the lure of entertainment and other worldly concerns, and the strength by which the bow is drawn is found in the lusts of the flesh and in the pride of life. When these twin powers are awakened and given preeminence over the influence of the spirit, the rockets of darkness are launched.

Satan has arrows trained at the hearts and minds of God's unhealthy children. Believers become spiritually sick at the initial slacking of their fervent devotion to God, for when we cease to occupy ourselves with Him, we cease to be healthy. The Lord uses the designs of darkness to bring forth the symptoms to show the child that he is sick. The Lord ensures that Satan's arrows never miss their targets; they always hit the unhealthy areas of our inner lives and cause them to flare up for detection. The Holy Spirit then quickly manifests the stricken areas to us through the knowledge of sin (Galatians 5:19-21).

Like Peter descending into the sea, the stricken believer in this moment must cry out to God in quick confession of his failure. Upon this confession, the conscience is once again sprinkled with the blood of Christ and the believer is brought back safely into the boat (Hebrews 10:22). Here, however, the designs of darkness attempt a new strategy. Upon seeing the believer is safe in Christ, the siren of false condemnation begins to sound.

Here, Christians who are not actively, methodically and untiringly resisting the onslaught of condemning thoughts will soon find themselves overrun and paralyzed and reeling off course. These impulses can be errantly theological and doctrinal in nature; they can be pornographic; they can be materialistic; they can be wrathful; they can be untrusting, doubting; they can be of bitterness, of unforgiveness or vengeance. These are all doorways for the powers of darkness to sink claws into the mind of a believer. But a Christian under the grace of the New Covenant has the power to reject all of these wicked invitations, and call on Jesus Christ the very moment they begin troubling the surface of his thoughts. (Matthew 8:25-26; II Corinthians 2:11;Ephesians4:26-27)

The Lord never removes Satan's invitations, but instead uses the power of grace to elevate us into positions of overcoming. Grace is the water by which God lifts us, like Noah, over all the mountains of temptation in the world. When God shut Noah in the boat, Noah died to the world and the world died to Noah.

Likewise, the overcoming Christian is he who is hid in Christ, the Ark of the New Covenant. What hill of gold is He not able to lift us above? What mountain of lust? What ridge of despair are we not able to transcend? As long as we are shut off from the world and dead in Him, there isn't a mountain in all of creation we cannot overcome. But without grace, we will never rise. Without grace, we will instead seek ways to go *through* the mountain instead of over it, to go around it instead of above it, and to dodge it rather than resist it. In all these scenarios, failure is assured. (Genesis 7:16-17; Galatians 6:14;Philippians4:13)

A defiled conscience coupled with a weak understanding of grace is a dangerous combination, for it puts a man in a raging sea without a life jacket, and in these situations it can be difficult to bring ourselves back into God's presence through the blood of Christ when our souls are downcast. The longer we hesitate to be restored, the heavier our sense of guilt becomes. The sirens of Satan will continue to broadcast that the blood alone is not sufficient, that we must "do" something additional to make an effective reconciliation, and that we are not who the Bible says we are in Christ. A hopeless sense of condemnation then sets in – while true justification and faith-charged restoration are but a confession away. (Romans8:15;Ephesians1:5;IJohn3:19-21)

When our spirits are depleted of grace, we

stop going forward and become sitting prey on the side of the narrow path for the enemy. This is why so many Christians live lives of chronic defeat and depression, despite all their Bible knowledge and Christian social activity. Inwardly they are poverty-stricken and starved of grace; their spirits are famished and too weak to rise. As a result, the enemy is able to have his way with their flesh and manipulate their thoughts. They need renewal!

Healthy Christians, on the other hand, are daily-renewed Christians, full of grace and victory in the Holy Spirit. They are able to pull their thoughts down into captivity and put Satan at flight every time he advances. They see themselves as living amidst an ever-flowing fountain of blood and grace. They are very careful in keeping watch over their minds and hearts. They are quick to confess secret sins and humble themselves in the inward parts. They cherish their Father's holiness and seek to be continuously filled and refilled with His Spirit to face the wicked challenge each day brings. (Matthew 7:13-14; II Corinthians 10:5; James4:7)

We must seek God for the daily renewal of our inner men to overcome sin in the moment-by-moment ordeals of temptation and spiritual warfare. We must have faith for this! If we come across a suggestive image, an impure thought, a piece of gossip, or an invitation to indecently amuse ourselves to the detriment to the life of God in us, we must turn our heads and flee from it as though it were a deadly virus!

A decision must be made each day to where we allow God to renew us in the spirit of our minds. Our value system must be realigned from the earthly to the eternal by resolving to take no thought for tomorrow and rest in His Word. The joy and relief that comes from this humble realignment is instant, but we must make this realignment quickly and not linger, lest Satan catch us off guard and trap us in our carnality. The heart can become so weighted-down with the pangs of condemnation that placing faith in the restorative efficacy of Christ's blood can seem an impossible task. May we therefore remain humble and attentive to the leading of the Spirit in keeping our minds renewed and hearts sanctified with all diligence. (Deuteronomy 4:9; Proverbs 4:23; 23:19; Ephesians 4:23; I Peter 3:15)

5. Beware of Preachers in Darkness

Preachers in darkness will come to you with real evangelical doctrines, with seminary knowledge of Greek and Hebrew, and with flowing exegesis delivered in spectacular eloquence. In all their eloquence, however, they will never tell you how difficult it is to enter through narrow way, or how few actually make through the gate. They'll instead widen it for everyone who says the sinner's prayer and acquiesces to an intellectual affirmation of the gospel. With all their dazzling oratory and mastery of hermeneutics you will not find one mention on how to overcome the lust of the eyes. They will teach you all about Joseph and his brothers in Egypt, but not how to overcome anger. They will teach you the proper Greek term for grace, but not how to be free from anxiety through grace. They'll explain to you the right contextual interpretation for Sheol and Hades in Scripture, but not how to triumph over the love of money and sexual addictions. And if they do speak of the crucifixion of the self-life, it is in high-brow, theological terms which cannot be practically assimilated by the common listener. (Matthew 7:13; I Corinthians 1:23; 2:4; Ephesians 4:14; Philippians 3:18; Colossians 2:8; Hebrews 13:9)

A preacher in darkness will extol the great praying exploits and Bible reading habits of dead saints, and unwittingly give Satan ammunition to bring you under condemnation. He will manipulate your emotions via soul-power to get you to tithe with the allurement of receiving an even greater reciprocal blessing from God (usually in the form of some earthly, financial dividend) to further feed your lust for money. A preacher in darkness will tell you only that the cross of Jesus Christ is God's means of forgiving your sins and improving the social, psychological and financial status of your life, but will not tell you that forgiveness of sin, healing, redemption from hell, and material prosperity were all available under the Old Covenant to any faithful Jew who obeyed the law (Psalm 103:3-5). You'll find no rain in the cloud to water you with the grace of Jesus Christ who actually delivers captives from *the inward power and tyranny of the flesh's nature* – a deliverance which no law-abiding, sacrifice-offering and tithing Jew could ever hope to experience under Moses. (Matthew 1:21; 6:6; John 1:17; II Corinthians 9:7; II Peter 2:17)

If secret lust still reigns in our hearts, we are enslaved. If our enthusiasm and great aspiration in life as Christians is only to make money and maximize our materialistic gain while on earth, we are deceived. It doesn't matter which church we attend, how well we know the Bible or how long we've been saved and filled with the Holy Spirit. A slave to sin is a slave to sin, no matter how correct his theology or how passionate his testimony. And a slave lives in darkness.

Scripture forewarns that the man who casts devils out of others but who does not allow Jesus to cast sin out of him, goes to hell; the man who heals the sick but who does not allow Jesus to heal the sickness of sin in him, is sent to hell; and the man who preaches the cross of Christ but who refuses to take it up himself cannot be a true follower of the Lord. We must not allow ourselves to be deceived by all the miracle and "deliverance" ministries of men and women who operate in the fiery prophetic but are yet in secret bondage themselves. If a ministry does not provoke you to reckon yourself dead to sin and daily take up the cross of self-death, such a ministry is a fraud no matter how gifted the preaching is, how many miracles are performed, demons cast out or people healed. (Matthew 7:21-23; Luke 14:27; John8:36;Romans6:18,20;IJohn2:4)

A great means by which the designs of darkness seek to deceive men and women through Christian preaching is found in the power of the soul. Deliverance occurs when the gospel is preached through the Holy Spirit; psychology occurs when it is preached through the soul. The vast majority of Christian ministry in the United States – both charismatic and non-charismatic – operates purely at the psychological level of intellect and emotion. Most preachers are unaware that they are being used by the forces of darkness through soul power, and so their listeners also cannot discern this usurpation due to the great emotional influence the soul has over their true spiritual condition. Through the employment of dynamically repetitious music, cadenced preaching and cerebral dissertations, multitudes of believers bereft of true Holy Spirit regeneration are made to feel sanctified, cleansed and justified on a weekly basis. The goal of this tactic is to deceive everyone into believing that real spiritual life is being proffered in the meeting, instead of just psychological blanks being fired into air. (Romans 16:18; Philippians 3:19; Colossians 2:8;Hebrews4:12)

Our eyes need to be opened to the truth that charged emotions and intellectual persuasions alone are incapable of bringing the Life of God into a dead vessel. This blessed transmittal can take place only within the confines of the quickened spirit. The spirit is the nucleus of the Life of Christ in a man, and if the Word of God does not vivify man's spirit with the transforming power of Jesus Christ, it will remain but dead psychology to the soul and mind. Feeding the soul with God's Word will inflate Bible knowledge and move the emotion, but it will not dismantle strongholds of addiction or break the power of the devil over one's life. (Romans 8:11; I Corinthians 8:1; 15:45; II Corinthians 3:6)

The divine provocation to surrender to the Holy Spirit in progressive measures of Christ-conformity is completely unavailable through the soul. The effects of soul are but transitory even under the greatest of preaching and ministry: in just a few days after a soul experience, the eyes will start lusting again, anger and impatience will re-flare, the anxiety and the cares of the world will return. Under even the most eloquent of soul-preaching, captives of sin soon discover the newly found freedom they thought they had was all but an illusion: the door to their freedom only led to a temporary reprieve in the prison courtyard.

In exchange for real spiritual freedom, the captive is made to feel loved in the prison. He is made to feel blessed, endued with special gifts, theologically adroit, and faithful on account of his weekly fellowship, volunteering for various tasks and in his paying of tithes and offerings (Jeremiah 6:14; 23:17; Ezekiel 13:10). Because the captives purport to feel the presence of the Lord through their preaching and music week after week, they conclude God is pleased with their walks. The reality, however, is that they are blinded by their own emotions and sit enslaved to sin in spiritual darkness. The Lord does not interfere and thus allows them to be defrauded by the wares of soul, resulting in the church's inability to differentiate between the worship leader and pastor's energy and the genuine ministry of the Holy Spirit. Satan's design for keeping a church in this condition is to prevent believers from seeking the grace of God to break the power of sin's dominion over their lives. (Ecclesiastes 8:11; Psalm 50:21)

Another tactic by which darkness prevails in keeping believers enslaved is by allowing them to think that being free from the power of sin equates to being in a state of sinless perfection (I John 1:8, 10). Multitudes are therefore deceived by this grand tactical design: they either congregate to one heretical camp which purports that they are without, and therefore cannot, sin; or to an opposite camp of cyclic defeat and forgiveness without any hope of ever overcoming sin's power and partaking of Christ's triumphant victory while on earth. Both camps continue to operate in darkness. (Philippians 3:13; Hebrews 6:1)

We must stop listening to the kind of

preaching which does not teach us how to overcome sin, but only causes us to be harder or softer on ourselves than God is. We must also beware of preachers who place a huge emphasis on radical prayer and Bible reading agendas, but who cannot teach believers from the Word with simplicity how to overcome sin and rejoice evermore. We must know how to tell the difference between Holy Spirit conviction and satanic condemnation in our journeys of sanctification. The Holy Spirit will never put a man on a guilt trip for not giving enough money, praying enough, or reading the Bible enough. The pressure to make these religious bricks comes from Pharaoh's taskmasters and never from God. Indeed, if we listen to such taskmasters we will find there is never an end to the bricks. The more bricks we make today, the more will be required tomorrow! (Exodus 5:8; Matthew 6:5-6;11:28;IThessalonians5:16)

Yet another tactic by which the powers of darkness seek to deceive believers through Christian ministry is to get them to concentrate on demonic "deliverance ministries" instead of sin-deliverance ministries. In truth, any type of deliverance ministry which does not deliver a man from sin is no deliverance ministry at all. Do not be deceived by those who equate the casting out of demons as true deliverance, for it is not. Many preachers with demon-deliverance ministries (and many believers who have had demons cast out of them) will only hear from

Jesus on the final day, *"I never knew you. Depart from me, you who practice sin"* (Matthew 7:22-23). If a preacher can only point out your sins but not teach you how to overcome them, he is wasting your time. If a preacher can only speak of forgiveness of sin but not deliverance from sin, he is wasting your time. If all a preacher can do is cast out devils and heal your body physically – but not teach you how to partake of Jesus' divine nature and consistently overcome sin through grace, such a preacher or teacher is not worth your attention.(Hebrews4:16;IIPeter1:4)

It is truly amazing how many faithful, church-attending Christians still do not know how to overcome the powers of darkness despite all the sermons they have heard and devotional materials they have read (II Timothy 3:7). Despite all their Bible knowledge and time in prayer most believers today remain totally defeated by sexual strongholds, by debate and strife, unending criticism, negativism, money worries and fear. And because of these strongholds, the Holy Spirit cannot operate through them to bring deliverance to others, nor can God trust them with His prophetic Word in their mouths or pen.

Such ministries and testimonies can only go as far as to touch the soul in pampering the intellect and stirring up the emotions. And this is the great deception. Any ministry which does not change you inwardly by provoking you to a greater surrender in humility, purity, sobriety and conformity to Jesus Christ is but a cloud without rain and a fire without light (Jeremiah 15:19; Proverbs 25:19; Jude 1:12).

6. Preventing the Invasions of Darkness

Scripture warns us that it is our duty to keep our hearts with all diligence, for the heart is susceptible to spiritual attack and can easily go after idols when not guarded. An unkept heart is like a moon without an atmosphere, a moon which has fallen prey to all the flying garbage of spiritual space. Without an atmosphere of grace, lustful temptations can strike the surface and cause all sorts of spiritual depressions through the conception of sin. (Proverbs4:23;IPeter3:15;IJohn5:21)

The designs of darkness target our minds and hearts daily with hostile thoughts and impure impulses. These spiritual trajectories seek to make deep impact and cause explosive damage to our walks with God. They aim to wound the conscience with the remembrance of sin and thus create a frustration in the obtainment of the grace of God (I John 3:21). God's grace is given to "keep" the heart from becoming overpowered by these attacks and to preserve the conscience from defilement through the partaking of Christ's nature.

Because of this, we must allow Christ to answer the door when strangers knock from the outside. We must be extremely careful when dealing with issues we know the powers of darkness are apt to steal our peace over; for example, we should always treat matters relating to money as though they were a loaded spring trap. Dealings with members of the opposite sex should be handled in identical fashion – with great trepidation and spiritual sobriety, with the believer ever-cognizant that these areas are often used as dangerous bait by the powers of darkness. God's Word exhorts us to abound in His grace so the shield of faith can continue to protect our hearts and minds from the bait through Christ Jesus.

We are not our own masters. We have been ransomed from hell by His blood; we must learn to find our rest and security in His protective grace (I Corinthians 6:20; 14:20; Philippians4:7; IPeter1:19). Before our rebirths, when we lived in the flesh to the fulfilling of our fleshly lusts, we were like orphaned moons in deep space without an atmosphere. We were alienated from God, full of darkness and void of protection. But Jesus rose from the dead and sent down the Holy Spirit to encompass our quickened spirits with grace and give us atmospheres to where the cosmic trajectories would no longer have dominion over us. We are no longer orphans lost in space - we are the ransomed sons and daughters of God and heirs to a Kingdom of eternal glory.

For the earnest of this promise, the Father has given us a foretaste of perfection through the filling, instruction and protection of the Holy Spirit. He indwells our bodies to make us more like Jesus through the exchange of the divine nature. He strengthens our inner men with might to shield us from the fiery trajectories of Satan: from the comets of lust, the meteors of pride and the discouragement of every evil design which can be conjured up and hurled at the surface of our hearts and minds (John 14:18; II Corinthians 1:22; Ephesians 2:3;6:16;Colossians1:21;James2:5).

But even here our spirits are not in a fixed state of strength. In the same way our physical bodies weaken if they do not eat and sleep, so our spiritual bodies also wane in strength when they are not rejuvenated through the Holy Spirit.

We are constantly winding down with fatigue as we confront the evil each day brings, and as we weaken in spirit, the world begins to regain momentum and a greater influence over our rebellious flesh. It is for this reason we are exhorted to make no provision for the flesh, but instead be renewed, transformed and purified in the spirit of our minds through obedience to God's Word. (Romans 13:14; Ephesians 3:16; I Peter1:22).

The result of a transformed mind is not in the removal of an obstacle, but in the lifting of us over it. This is the principle of overcoming. Many Christians expect God to remove their problems. As a result, such Christians never enter into the New Covenant life of perpetual triumph. Ironically, the things God *does* desire to take away – the love of money, the secret lust of the eyes, the boast of life – are often the very things we do not want to give up. These He delights in taking away, but when it comes to our own inconveniences and trials His way is to rather lift us above and over them, thus building our faith through resistance and mortification (James 1:2-4; II Peter 1:5-8).

Since the flesh's vibrancy is hostile to the health of our inner men, it must be put down to prevent a war. The designs of darkness deliberately spur the flesh to rise in battle against the spirit to damage the conscience. But God shows Christians how to stay strong in their inner men by remaining connected to the grace of His Spirit. The moment we separate from His power, we become like fish pulled from the sea. Humility keeps us safe in the sea of His grace, for it is in this sea where our spirits receive restorative life and new power. (John15:5;Galatians5:17)

We lose our abode in this blessed place of life and protection when we grow proud. This is because God resists the proud, for pride is an indicator of the inward flex of our satanic nature's rebellion and self-sufficiency through our eating from the tree of knowledge. Pride is antithetical to grace, for God's power is perfected in our weakness, dependency and humility. His grace is frustrated the moment we begin boasting in ourselves.

The moment we begin to think we are entitled to some fleshly merit or acclaim, grace withdraws from our spirits, the protective atmosphere vanishes, and God Himself begins to resist us. What does this resistance mean? When we neglect the keeping of our hearts in humble correspondence with the Holy Spirit, God Himself denies our efforts in combating temptation and leaves us graceless to fall to the bullies of darkness. The very power we need to overcome and survive the Christian life is taken away and all of our independent efforts in gaining it back are resisted. Our minds soon become invaded with strongholds, and ultimately we can come to believe error through a seared conscience. (Job 5:13; Isaiah 2:11; Obadiah 1:3; II Thessalonians 2:11; James 4:6)

When we do not repent of pride and come back into a right standing of humility before the Father, the results can be tragic. As already mentioned, one such tragedy can come through a seared conscience (I Timothy 4:2). The Bible teaches that the conscience of man is allied to the Word of God (Romans 2:15), but when a person continually rejects the Holy Spirit's reprimand to his sin, the signals of his conscience can become cauterized to where they no longer sound an alarm to the spirit (Romans 1:28; Ephesians 4:19; II Thessalonians 2:11). Sin's power becomes an executioner's hood placed upon the head of the conscience, and the deceived victim is hanged by the rope of his own pride.

To keep the voice of our conscience strong and pure, we must seek to remain humble at all times by taking the "lower seat" at the feasts of life, by counting others as more important than ourselves, and by the immediate confession of all our failures to God, no matter how slight or hidden they may seem. Humility begets grace, grace begets victory over sin, victory over sin begets a pure heart, a pure heart begets the anointing of God upon one's life, and when God's power rests on a man there is a great temptation for him to become proud – and thus the Christian's cycle of life in the school of God runs full circle as he again surrenders to the death of the cross to obtain grace. (Proverbs25:6;Luke14:10;Philippians2:3)

When the conscience becomes seared, the natural response of man is to begin pushing God out of his life altogether (Romans 1:23). When men no longer embrace God's estimation of sin – that is, in His indictment of their satanic nature which renders them all to be in dead in sin and thus alienated from Him but by the blood atonement of Christ – when men love not the truth of these sovereign decrees, God gives them over to embrace all sorts of deception and abominable practices as they speed their way into the outer darkness of eternal separation and hellfire. He will allow, for example, the pride of human intellect to marry the flesh and create systems of atheism and evolution; He will allow the deceived soul to come into union with the flesh and give birth to various false religious systems, metaphysics and fraudulent mysticism. The designs of darkness bring these shrouds of deception to further buttress man's independence from God. In all of these satanic designs, for both the religious and irreligious alike, a deceived man is blissfully free to pursue his heart's desires without acquiescing that he is a slave to sin and a captive of Satan. His eyes will be opened to the horror of this truth after his mortal demise. (2Corinthians4:4;2Timothy2:26;Hebrews9:27)

To learn something about the rudiments of the New Covenant Christian life, we can take a lesson from a dead person reposing in a casket. Where are his rights, his earthly ambitions? They are gone, for he is now passed. Where is his boast of life? It is gone, for he has now passed. Where is his reaction to men's praises and criticisms? All is silent, for he has passed. Where are his worries of the stock market and rising gas prices? They are no more, for he has passed. Drop a bag of ten million dollars on his chest and yet he will not move. Let pornography or fear try to draw him out of the coffin, but he still cannot be stirred to life, for he has passed. We too are called to *reckon ourselves* to be the same as this dead man, dead in our caskets of Christ, crucified and loathsome to the world. The world, in turn, must become the same dead, grotesque thing to us. Anything less than real death in Christ leading to eternal life is not true Christianity, but fraudulent life in Adam leading to eternal death. For in Adam life is death, but in Christ death is life. The designs of darkness work to convince man of the exact opposite. (Romans 6:6;Galatians6:14;Colossians3:3)

Satan is able to strike your mind in such a way as to paralyze all your theology and knowledge of the Bible in an instant. We must make sure that our abiding is not in a shadow, but in the Reality which casts it. Therefore, when Satan comes to you, he should find you dead. He should find you crucified with Christ and hid in God, dead to the world, dead to sin, dead to the lusts of the flesh, with all your earthly members, including your tongue and thoughts, mortified and nailed to the cross. For a corpse cannot be stirred; a corpse cannot be made to gossip, chase money, become depressed, lose its patience or sexually fantasize. When the tempter comes, he should find nothing but a naked corpse hanging limp on a cross. It's too late. (John 14:30; 16:33; Romans 6:7)

A decision must be made anew each morning to where the Christian has determined to yield the entire day to the death-cross of Jesus Christ. His tongue, his eyes, his mind all must be nailed to the wood. Much emphasis has been placed on Bible reading and prayer as first-thing-in-the-morning imperatives, but these activities will bear lasting fruit only when they are done in the blessed aftermath of this daily resolution. Our morning prayers must rise as incense above the altar of our own sacrificial deaths in Christ, and all our Bible reading must take place only after we've committed the deliberate mortification of our own self-will into His Hands. (Luke 23:46; Philippians 2:5-8)

7. Darkness Defeated through Humility

"The Lord will fight for you, and you shall hold your peace" (Exodus 14:14).

When we are not overcoming darkness, darkness is overcoming us. This is a universal law set in motion by God, and cannot be changed. Light always triumphs over darkness, and the two are forever at odds; but it is the darkness which is sneakily opportunistic in filling voids when the strength of the light begins to abate. Impure lust, discouragement, the love of money, anxiety, jealousy, greed, hypocrisy, gluttony, anger, impatience, disbelief, self-acclaim, malice, fear - the child of God faces all these inward giants with his shield raised, sword-in-fist and teeth clenched as they wreak havoc on his devotion life, family life and daily affairs. The question must therefore be asked: has the Christian soldier been left alone on the battlefield to be vanquished by these giants with nothing in his defense but forgiveness, or is the grace of God available for him to systematically tread upon all their necks in victory? If you have resigned your soul to an endless cycle of defeat and forgiveness, then I believe you have missed the most wonderful aspect of your birthright in Christ. Like Esau, a lying Jacob has used a carnal morsel to cheat you out of your inheritance. (Genesis 25:29-34; Joshua10:24-25;Hebrews12:16)

Do not let Satan rob you anymore. You can overcome them all! Shall I say it again? *You can overcome all the designs of darkness, all the corruption of the world, and all the battles of the flesh through Christ whereby you are made more than a conqueror.* The real Christian life is one of perpetual victory. Daily deliverance from sin's power is your New Covenant birthright; Jesus Christ is your Great Deliverer by faith. If you are yet expecting to be delivered from sin through the efforts of self-determination and religious willpower, a thousand years will go by and you will still be defeated. You will go to your grave having never tasted of the glorious triumph over sin offered to you though the death and resurrection of the Lord Jesus Christ (Romans 8:31-39; 11:26; II Corinthians 2:14; Colossians 1:13; I Thessalonians 1:10; II Timothy 4:18).

Most believers seem to have only grasped

the rudimentary message of forgiveness of sin, when the essential message of the gospel of Jesus Christ is one of *deliverance from sin* and Satan's power. As a result, most Christians go up and down in cycles of excitement and depression, happiness and anxiety, victory and defeat. They know they can experience forgiveness of sin through Christ, but on how to actually overcome these sins they are powerless.

Most Christians think that memorizing scripture, fasting or prolonged prayer will somehow better equip them with this power. The devil would have them remain ignorant to the secret of total freedom from sin's enslavement, and instead only regard the cross of Jesus Christ as a means of forgiveness after defeat. They need the revelation that Jesus is their Great Deliverer! Most Christians do not understand that His death disarmed Satan and took away the power of sin's dominion from the soul of redeemed man. This is tremendously good news! It means all the designs of darkness have already been vanquished through the cross – and we, as God's children and heirs to His Kingdom, are now free to walk in our triumphant inheritance by the faith and merit of God's Son. (John 8:36; 12:31; 16:11; Galatians3:3;Colossians2:15)

We are now able to overcome sin's dominion as we yield ourselves to the Holy Spirit through death. This death-reckoning is wholly by faith and precludes any type of human effort, psychology or fleshly reformation. We can never in a million years hope to win a spiritual battle by our own faculties of the will, by relying on the arm of flesh! David wielding King Saul's sword, gritting his teeth and charging Goliath on the battlefield is a picture of suicidal lunacy! David's defeat in this case is certain. But this is the same idiotic mission we undertake when we attempt to fight the hosts of darkness without God's grace. The designs of darkness can be combated only through drawing back of the sling of the Cross and sending forth the Rock of Ages, the Life of God's Son, into the face of the enemy. As we stand fast, clad in all God's spiritual weaponry and armor, Christ's victory is always certain. (Galatians 5:16; Ephesians 6:10-18;ISamuel17:38-51)

It is only when we attempt to do battle by the sword of psychology and humanistic effort where we doom ourselves to perpetual defeat. We should never try to change ourselves in God's school, for God will not accept the change even if we are able; we must instead allow Him to make the change in us, and give Him the time to do it. Our duty is only to keep our consciences clear by continually confessing, loathing and forsaking sin. Our task is simply to collaborate with the Holy Spirit in yielding. When Satan brings ungodly thoughts to our minds, we must be able to instantly say, *"This fight is not for me"* and fly to Christ for grace to overcome. If we take the time to do this, we will find Him faithful each time in providing a way out of the temptation. (I Corinthians10:13;James4:7;Hebrews2:18)

We must learn to call upon the Lord the very moment we are tempted, for He is our *"present"* source of refuge (Psalm 46:1). As we presently call upon Him for victory, we will see the waters open and swallow the temptation before our eyes. He will deliver us yet again from the tyranny of sin, and cause us to rejoice evermore upon the seashore of our sojourning. We can triumph every time if we only learn to humble ourselves and resign the fight to the Lord's hands. When the tyrant of temptation comes for us in the iron chariot, God will make an escape route through the Red Sea of Christ's blood.

If we would know the secret of God's strength in battle, we must first know the truth of our weakness. The real Christian life is one of victory authored by the Strong living though the weak. The way to defeat the designs of darkness is through the humility of our own confessed insufficiencies. This means we must never make an outward expression which contradicts our inward reality. God's grace to transform us comes always by way of humility, by stripping off the mask. If we would be victors in Christ we must never seek to gain man's approval at the expense of cloaking this honesty. The nature of Christ living through man is what makes him more than a conqueror, and hence, the man who puts on Christ need never lose his peace, joy or his confidence in victory –for all these are Christ's.

Christ has defeated Satan! Christ has overcome the world! Christ has risen from the dead! When the same Spirit which raised Christ from the dead inhabits our mortal bodies, we too shall partake of His divine nature and the life of God will instantly elevate us to positions of supernatural conquest. (Rom.8:11;13:14;ICor.1:30;IICorinthians12:10; Ephesians2:14;Colossians1:27)

Dear Christian, you have read this book thus far, and are serious about your walk. Are you now prepared to step into your birthright which renders you to be more than a conqueror through Christ? Learn then to yield to the leadings of the Holy Spirit, beginning in your thought life. Take time to be holy in your thoughts, for holiness is a habit. Give the Holy Spirit free reign to begin overseeing and controlling your mind. Allow Him to regulate your thoughts and do not resist His dealings of death to your flesh. This will take time and be very painful at the onset, but you will soon come to kiss the very cross upon which God is slaying you, for it will be the blessed instrument by which Life of Christ is exalted in you through the humility of death (Philippians 2:8-9). The humbling of ourselves unto the death of the cross is the magnificent secret by which the overcoming grace of God enters our spirits.

Start by gently turning away from sinful impressions when they are first presented to you, by confessing in your heart, *"This is sin. This is not for me."* God will see that you are serious in forsaking sin and equip you with supernatural grace to resist and overcome. As a result of this, your heart will remain pure, your conscience undefiled, your faith will build and ceaseless prayer will rise like incense from your spirit to His (Psalm 141:2; Revelation 5:8). You will then enter into a peaceful rest that surpasses all knowledge. The Lord will begin to give you powerful revelation in His Word that relates to your sanctification and bless you with wisdom and a genuine compassion for hurting people.

You will have discovered the pearl of great price, and will happily give all you have for it, for you will see that all the knowledge, wisdom, riches and beauty on earth is but dung and garbage in comparison. Satan does not want you operating within this realm, which is why this book is predicated upon overcoming his designs through grace. (Matthew 13:46; John 14:27;Philippians2:4;3:8;4:7)

Perhaps you have been taught that victory over sin is not possible in this life. This is a lie of darkness, a design of Satan. You can have victory as you lay hold of God's New Covenant promise through faith. You must come to the place where you can claim every promise in the New Testament pertaining to spiritual joy, victory, overcoming sin, grace, triumph, perfection, humility, meekness and godliness, and then have faith that God will actuate every single one of them in your life. Most defeated believers will not believe God's Word, but rather cling to a form of godliness which denies His power. As a result, the vast majority of Christians do not reckon themselves as dead. They remain alive in the vanity of their thought lives, in their memories of past failures, and in the recollections their dysfunctional childhoods and abusive relationships. The pride of the flesh will not let these things go, and so God allows them suffer under demonic oppression and strongholds. And here they will die, unless they at last come to their senses and throw in the white towel of surrender. (Habakkuk 2:4; IICor.5:7;Philippians3:13-15;IITimothy3:5)

Once a man reckons himself as dead in Christ and thus unable to further defend, justify or sanctify himself, he will begin to actuate by faith a spiritual reality which occurred eons ago when God crucified him in Christ. When we cease from all our fighting to preserve our fleshly ambition and dignity, when we consign to the grave all our past regrets and tragedies, and when we come at last see ourselves as deceased in the casket of Christ, and laying in blessed repose from the power of sin (realizing that God crucified our "old man" in Christ so that the body of sin would be destroyed and hold no more dominion over us), the law of the Spirit of Life in Christ will supernaturally come into effect whereby we will be able transcend all the designs of spiritual darkness. We will have entered into the grace of the New Covenant. (Romans6:6;8:2;ICor.1:30;Philippians3:3)

This enabling power is proffered upon us only as we enter into our identity and personal humility in Jesus Christ's death. *We must die for this grace.* We must settle all our delinquent accounts on this earth, forgive whomever we need to forgive, close out all our spiritual debts, forever relinquish all our secret ambitions and entitlements to this life, and go to God and die. The moment we see ourselves as dead is the moment the earth will quake and the rocks of our cyclic defeats will break. The prison door of our strongholds will be flung wide open and we, the captives of sin, will be set free. (Acts 16:25-34; Romans 13:8; I Corinthians15:31,50)

All the designs of Satan are defeated through death, and the Lord shows us how to stay dead through the systematic mortification of our members on earth. When we can come to see the blood of Christ as an ever-flowing fountain beneath which we abide and fellowship with God in the Light, continuously purifying the conscience and building our faith through grace, the Spirit of the Living God will then burst forth from our bellies to water other hurting believers and point them to the same place of death and total deliverance from whence we came. Oh praise God! The Christian life is a glorious life, full of power and freedom and joy! A foretaste of Heaven on earth! (Proverbs 11:25; John 7:38; Colossians1:12-13;3:5)

The greatest secret to all growth in the Christian life is *humility*. A Christian's walking in humility is the grand design by which all the designs of the devil are defeated. A humble man or woman receives immediate light on every area of their life which falls short of God's glory, and with this light, the accompanying grace to set it right and continue on to perfection. Ask God right now to begin the process of fostering Christ's divine nature in your life and then come to the Master with all your weakness and failure and misery. His only requirement from you is poverty in spirit and a thirst to have your heavy burden of sin-enslavement removed. He will then begin doing what you have tried for so many years but failed to do. The Goliaths will fall. Your life will change.

A river is waiting to flow from your bosom, and God is impartial through whom it proceeds, for He gives abundant grace to all who call on Him in true humility. (Proverbs 11:2; 15:33; 22:4; Matthew 5:3; Acts 10:34; I Corinthians 3:18; II Corinthians 3:5; Colossians 3:12; I Peter 5:6)

ABOUT THE AUTHOR

Paul West, author of *"Understanding Mortification"* and *"Designs of Darkness"* holds an AAS in mortuary science from San Antonio College and is a dual-licensed funeral director and embalmer in the state of Texas. Mr. West is also a forum moderator for *Sermon Index,* a website dedicated to the propagation Christ-centered revival, for which he's written hundreds of essays and articles dealing with overcoming sin, spiritual warfare and the deeper Christian life. He and his wife Marissa live in San Marcos, Texas with their two children.

He can be reached at: *pwest@centurytel.net*

Proof

18843240R00040

Made in the USA
Charleston, SC
23 April 2013